UKRAINE

MOLDOVA

Cernovcy

Botoşani

Suceava

Moldova

Bahlui

Iaşi

Prut

Chişinău

M O L D A V I A

Piatra-Neamţ

Vaslui

Bacău

Miercurea-Ciuc

COVASNA

Sfântu Gheorghe

Siret

Focşani

Braşov

Galaţi

Sinaia

Brăila

Danube Delta

Prahova

Buzău

Tulcea

Târgovişte

Ploieşti

Black Sea

Dâmboviţa

Slobozia

Ialomiţa

BUCHAREST

Dunăre

Mamaia

Danube-Black Sea Canal

Constanţa

Călăraşi

Costineşti

LACHIA

Danube

Mangalia

xandria

Giurgiu

Ruse

BULGARIA

Romania

an Willem Bos

A Cherrytree Book

This edition published in 2009 by Evans Brothers Limited
2A Portman Mansions
Chiltern Street
London W1U 6NR, UK

Published by arrangement with KIT Publishers, The Netherlands

Copyright © 2009 KIT Publishers – Amsterdam

British Library Cataloguing-in-Publication Data
Bos, Jan Willem.
   Romania. -- (New EU countries and citizens)
   1. Romania--Juvenile literature.
   I. Title II. Series
   949.8-dc22
ISBN-13: 9781842345856

Text: Jan Willem Bos
Translation: Shannon Davidson
UK editing: Sonya Newland
Book design: Miranda Zonneveld, Alkmaar
Cover: Big Blu Ltd
Cartography: Armand Haye, Amsterdam, The Netherlands

Picture Credits
All images courtesy of Jan Willem Bos, except the following:
Benjamin Gantikov: 21t; Jo Goossens: 22t, 25t, 26t&m, 39t, 40t; André Kom: 3, 16m;
Aad Littooij: 11b; Manfred Wirtz: 37m.

Contents

4 Introduction

5 History

12 Country

16 Cities

22 Transport

25 People

31 Education

35 Cuisine

39 Economy

43 Tourism

46 Nature

48 Glossary and Index

▲ *The brand new bank building mirrors the old savings bank next to it.*

Introduction

On 29 March 2004 Romania became a member of the military alliance NATO, and on 1 January 2007 it joined the European Union (EU). Both these events were significant for the Romanian people who, after years of being isolated in Eastern Europe, now feel that they belong to the West again.

From the end of the Second World War until 1989, Romania was under the influence of the Soviet Union and was a communist country. There was only one political party – the Communist Party of Romania – and all factories and shops were owned by the state. People were imprisoned or exiled from Romania if they publicly disagreed with the politics of the Communist Party. In December 1989, the people of Romania revolted against the communist dictatorship and the controlling party leader, Nicolae Ceausescu, was overthrown, setting the country on the road to democracy.

Freedom and democracy

Since Romania has become free and democratic again, much has changed. People are allowed to express political views without fear of reprisal, free elections are held and all state-owned companies have been replaced by private ones. Many new houses, businesses and motorways are being built.

Unfortunately though, not everyone has been able to profit from the improved political and economic circumstances. There is still a lot of poverty in rural areas as well as in the cities. As salaries are low compared to countries such as Britain, many Romanians go abroad to work. They take temporary jobs as farm workers, or work on construction sites or as cleaners. Many Romanian doctors and engineers leave their country because they can earn 10 times more in Western Europe or the USA than they can in Romania.

A new challenge

Now that Romania is a member of the EU, the speed of change and development has started to increase. This also means that the country has to face new challenges. The often primitive farming methods will have to be modernised, with the risk that many people will lose their jobs and income. However, as a member of the EU, it will be easier for Romania to face these challenges. After half a century of communist rule and the often difficult transition to democracy, most Romanians feel that better times lie ahead.

▼ *Turkeys gather under the watchful eye of a farmer's dog.*

History

Romania has had a turbulent history, and the country's borders as they are today have only existed since the end of the Second World War in 1945.

▲ The Romanian coat of arms: an eagle with a cross in its mouth. The coat of arms also shows the various provinces of Romania.

In the past, Romania had three main principalities: Wallachia, Moldavia and Transylvania. The history of Transylvania – known as Siebenbürgen ('seven fortresses') in German – is very different from that of Wallachia and Moldavia.

The Roman period and the Middle Ages

Two thousand years ago a huge empire called Dracia covered the area that is now Romania. This region was ruled by Decabalus (reigned AD 87–106). The Roman emperor, Trajan, saw Dacia as a threat to the Roman Empire, and between AD 101 and AD 106 he carried out two campaigns to conquer the region. After the defeat of the Dacians and the death of Decebalus, the Dacian territory was occupied by colonists from all over the Roman Empire. They spoke Latin – the language from which Romanian derives. A century and a half later, because of the threat of hostile barbarians on the north-eastern borders, the Roman emperor decided to give up the principality and withdraw the Roman army and government south of the River Danube.

◀ This map of Dacia by Claudius Ptolemy dates from the second century BC).

During this time, known as the Migration Period, many nomadic tribes – among them the Huns and the Goths – moved through the region that is now Romania. The Hungarians, or Magyars, came from Asia and settled in the north-west of the Carpathian Mountains in the area called Transylvania. There are very few written documents from this time, so it is difficult to establish exactly what happened in the period between the Roman withdrawal and the time when the first Romanian states, Wallachia and Moldavia, were established in the thirteenth and fourteenth centuries. It is said that 1,000 years are missing from the history of Romania.

▶ The medieval church of Densuş dates from the thirteenth century.

The king of darkness, the undead Transylvanian vampire count who sinks his teeth into the necks of his victims and drinks their blood, did not originate in Romanian folklore but in the imagination of the Irish writer Bram Stoker, who published his famous novel *Dracula* in 1897. Stoker was probably inspired by the medieval vampire stories and pictures of Vlad Draculea (or Dracula, 1431–76). Dracula was very cruel and was famous for killing his enemies by impaling them on wooden pikes. He was given the nickname Vlad Tepes, which means 'Vlad the Impaler'. For the Romanians he was also a national hero because he fought fiercely against the Turks, who were trying to seize Romanian lands. However, Dracula is better known than Vlad, and an enormous number of films and cartoons have been made about the character in Stoker's book, including Francis Ford Coppola's film *Bram Stoker's Dracula*. There are plans to build an amusement park called Dracula Land in Romania.

▲ *A fifteenth-century portrait of Count Dracula.*

▶ *A letter dating from* AD *152, from the merchant Neacsu to the mayor of Kronstadt (now Brasov), is the oldest preserved document in the Romanian language. It is written using the Cyrillic (Slavonic) alphabet.*

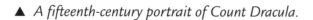

Ottoman rule

Wallachia and Moldavia were small countries and quickly came under the influence of a powerful neighbour: the Empire of the Ottoman Turks. To prevent being occupied by the Ottomans, the two countries paid huge sums of money to the Turkish sultan and also paid him in agricultural products.

Throughout its history the people of Romania frequently fought against the Turkish threat. During the fifteenth century, the Moldavian king Stephen the Great ruled for 48 years and fought 40 battles against the Turks; he won 38 of them. In 1600, Michael the Brave of Wallachia (ruled 1596–1601) managed – for a short while – to unite the three principalities of Wallachia, Moldavia and Transylvania for the first time. He is considered a great national hero by the Romanians.

◀ *This statue of Mihai Viteazul (Michael the Brave) stands in the centre of Bucharest. It is customary to meet at the 'horse's tail'.*

The Phanariots

At the start of the eighteenth century another powerful neighbouring country, Russia, gained more influence in the Romanian principalities. To strenghthen their control in Wallachia and Moldavia, the Turks put people on the throne that they could trust – high-ranking Greek officials who were in the service of the sultan. Because they came from the Phanar in Constantinople (now Istanbul), they were called Phanariots. They ruled the Romanian principalities until 1821 when the Romanians, led by Tudor Vladimirescu, revolted against their Greek and Turkish oppressors. The uprising was quickly suppressed and Vladimirescu was killed. The Romanians, however, partly got what they wanted: Wallachia and Moldavia were governed once more by Romanian rulers.

National awareness

Transylvania had been part of the kingdom of Hungary since the eleventh century. In the seventeenth century, both Transylvania and Hungary came under the rule of the Austrian Habsburgs. Transylvania remained part of the Habsburg Empire until 1918. Half the population in Transylvania was made up of Romanians, but they had no rights and their Orthodox Christian religion was not recognised. A Romanian nationalist movement, called the 'Transylvanian School', came into being in the eighteenth century. The members of the movement thought it unfair that only Germans and Hungarians had a say in important matters in their territory and they asked the Austrian emperor to grant them equal rights. Although they failed, the movement raised awareness of the plight of the Romanians in the empire.

The Union of Wallachia and Moldavia

In the nineteenth century, the Romanians started to view the West – and especially France – as a model for how their own country could be. The people in the towns threw off their Eastern habits and clothing and were inspired by the ideas of the French revolution: 'freedom, equality and brotherhood'.

In 1848, progressive groups tried to introduce a liberal constitution and social reforms. At the same time, they tried to rid themselves of their Turkish rulers and Russian interference. Once again, they failed, but the attempts had sown the seeds of an idea that Romanians should all live together in one country.

In 1859, Colonel Alexandru Ioan Cuza was chosen as ruler of the United Principalities of Wallachia and Moldavia. Although the union was only intended to last for Cuza's period of government, it lasted and the name Romania was taken for this united nation.

▶ Alexandru Ioan Cuza (1820–73), prince of the United Principalities of Wallachia and Moldavia.

Independence

After Cuza, in 1866, the united principalities found themselves under the leadership of a German head of state – King Carol von Hohenzollern-Sigmarinen. For the first time in its history, Romania was granted a constitution, based on that used in Bulgaria, which was considered very forward-thinking and modern.

Romania was a very poor and undeveloped country at the time, but in the 48 years of Carol I's rule it developed and modernised quickly. During the Russian-Turkish War of 1877–78, Romania fought with Russia and used the Russian victory to declare itself completely free of Turkey. The conflict became known in Romania as the War of Independence.

Between 1828 and 1914, Romania grew more stable and progressive. However, the majority of Romanians were still farmers who often lived in great poverty. In 1907, the Peasant's Revolt against the wealthy landowners was violently suppressed. Thousands of peasants died during the revolt.

▶ *King Carol I.*

The First World War

When the First World War broke out in 1914, Romania remained neutral. In 1916, however, the country joined forces with France and England, which had promised to return Transylvania to the Romanians if they fought against Germany and Austria. On 1 December 1918, the Romanian inhabitants of Transylvania – the majority of the population – declared themselves in favour of unification. The day is still celebrated as a national holiday in Romania. The Hungarians who lived in Transylvania preferred to remain with Hungary, but the German Transylvanian people chose to belong to Romania rather than to Hungary.

The country that resulted from this unification was known as Great Romania. It was almost twice the size of the kingdom of Romania before 1914.

▶ *Unity Square in Timosoara is named after the unification of the three Romanian monarchies.*

Just like in many European countries, after the First World War Romania erected a monument to 'The Unknown Soldier' – one of the many soldiers who died during the war and whom nobody could identify. In May 1923, 10 coffins were dug up containing the bodies of unknown Romanian soldiers from which a soldier was to be chosen. A Romanian schoolboy and war orphan, Amilcar C. Sandulescu, was asked which of the 10 would receive the place of honour in the grave of the Unknown Soldier. He knelt in front of the fourth coffin and said: 'This is my father.' The coffin he had chosen was taken to Bucharest and buried with military honours.

▲ *Stamps issued on the fiftieth anniversary of the unification of Transylvania with the rest of Romania.*

Great Romania

In the interwar period, Romania industrialised rapidly, and its population expanded. At the same time, it suffered from the economic depression being felt all over the world at the beginning of the 1930s. One result of this was that an extreme nationalistic movement came into being. Called the Iron Guard, members of this movement only wanted 'real' Romanians – not foreigners or Jews – to have power in the country. They were not afraid of using violence to press their ideas home. In 1938, King Carol II introduced a royal dictatorship and banned all political parties. This meant the end of Romanian parliamentary democracy for the next 50 years.

▲ *Bucharest in the interwar years.*

◄ *When this 100-Leu banknote was issued in 1947, Romania was not yet a people's republic, but the design already shows signs of the coming communism.*

The Second World War

At the beginning of the Second World War, in 1939, Romania again remained neutral. However, Germany and Russia forced the country to relinquish some of its land. A large part of Transylvania was subsumed into Hungary, and northern and eastern Moldavia were annexed by the Soviet Union. The unpopular King Carol II was forced to abdicate and his son Mihai came to the throne. Real power, though, lay with the military dictator General Ion Antonescu. To win back the lost territories, Antonescu forced Romania to join the war on the German side. On 23 August 1944, when it became clear that Germany was losing, King Mihai had Antonescu arrested and Romania switched sides. After the war, the country regained Transylvania, but eastern Moldavia remained part of the Soviet Union. When the Soviet Union collapsed in 1991, this area became an independent country: the Republic of Moldavia.

The communist era

At the end of the Second World War in 1945, Romania was occupied by the army of the communist Soviet Union. Despite the fact that very few Romanians supported communism, the following year the Communist Party rigged the election and came to power. Democratic political parties were banned and their leaders were thrown into prison. On 30 December 1947, King Mihai was forced to abdicate and the People's Republic of Romania was proclaimed. Anyone who opposed the regime was imprisoned or deported.

For more than a decade, Romania – like other communist countries in Eastern Europe – was largely cut off from the West. In the 1960s, however, relations with Western countries began to improve. In 1965, Nicolae Ceausescu became the leader of the Communist Party; he was an independent thinker and at first he was popular in the West as well as in Romania itself.

Also called the House of the People, the Palace of the Parliament is the second largest building in Europe and the second largest in the world after the Pentagon. A 150-m wide road (officially called the Boulevard of the Victory of Socialism, but known as the Boulevard of the Draughts) led to the palace. Only Romanian materials were used in its construction and interiors: 2,800 chandeliers, 22,000 sq m of carpet, 3,445 tonnes of crystal, 3,500 sq m of leather, more than 3 million sq m of marble and many tonnes of wood. The palace cost around £3 billion to build. When the December Revolution took place in 1989, the palace was not yet finished so Ceausescu never got to enjoy his life's work. The first person to wave to the crowds from the central balcony was not Ceausescu but the singer Michael Jackson. After the fall of communism, parliament started to use the building, changing its name to the Palace of the Parliament.

Over the following years, however, it became clear that Ceausescu wished to rule the country as a dictator. He pursued a disastrous economic policy and oppressed the population with the help of the Securitate – the feared secret police. While Ceausescu was building a huge palace in Bucharest, the Romanian people were going hungry. This period has become known as the era of the three f's: *foame, frica, frig* ('hunger, fear, cold'). At the same time, Ceausescu distributed propaganda in which he called himself 'the genius of the Carpathians' and 'the most loved son of the people'. Television programmes educated people about his 'great deeds' and those of his wife, Elena.

▼ *The Palace of the Parliament in Bucharest.*

Investim în oameni.

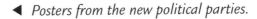
Posters from the new political parties.

Revolution and transition

In 1989, communist regimes all over Eastern Europe began to collapse as the people revolted against the oppression and poverty they had lived with since the end of the Second World War. In most cases, these revolutions took place without violence, but in Romania it was a different story. In December 1989, a successful but violent uprising took place against Ceausescu and his communist government. Around 1,000 people died, among them many schoolchildren and students who had bravely protested against the dictatorship. Ceauaescu and his wife were executed by a firing squad on Christmas Day 1998.

Now that the communists had been overthrown, Romania was a free country. There was no longer any censorship, democratic political parties could be set up again and free elections held. A few years after the revolution, all political parties agreed to do their best to move Romania towards becoming a member of NATO and the European Union, which they believed would improve Romania's status in Europe.

The years after the fall of communism were not easy. Many people found the transition chaotic and were disappointed by how slowly reforms seemed to take place. While some businessmen became extremely wealthy, many Romanians – especially the unemployed, elderly and handicapped – remained very poor. Some people even felt that life had been better under the communist regime.

In the years between the fall of communism and Romania's entry into the European Union, a lot changed in the country. It is no longer a dictatorship with a state-led economy, but a parliamentary democracy with an economy led by private enterprise. There is political and economic freedom and Romanians can travel throughout Europe without a visa. However, half a century of communism has left problems that will take longer to resolve.

Despite this, Romania has a bright future as a member of the European Union and of NATO. There is more wealth now than ever before, and ordinary people are beginning to feel the benefits of the improved economy. The fact that they belong to the West again is very important to the Romanians, who have always felt that Romania is a Western country.

▶ *There is press freedom again in Romania since the fall of communism.*

▲ *A cow looks out of a barn on this Romanian farmstead.*

Country

Romania (in Romanian 'România', with the emphasis on the 'î') lies in the middle of Europe. It borders Hungary in the north-west (447 km), the Ukraine (694 km) in the north and east, the Republic of Moldavia (681 km) in the north-east, Bulgaria (631 km) in the south and Serbia (546 km) in the south-west.

Romania's coastline along the Black Sea in the east runs for 193 km. The River Danube forms the southern border with Serbia and Bulgaria, and has a length of 750 km. The distance between London and Bucharest is about 2,089 km – which means it takes around three and a half hours to fly between these two cities.

Town and countryside

Romania is a medium-sized country, the thirteenth largest in Europe. It covers 238,393 sq km, which is slightly larger than the UK. In 2007, Romania had a population of approximately 21.5 million, which makes it the tenth most populated country in Europe.

Around two million people – 10 per cent of the population – live in the capital Bucharest. However, Bucharest's population is usually much higher than this, as the city draws many temporary workers who live there for a while and then move on. Although many factories were built in the cities during the communist era, which attracted many people there to find work, half the Romanian population still lives in rural areas, in around 13,000 villages scattered across the country.

While many old buildings have been torn down to make way for blocks of flats in the cities, most villages have kept their traditional feel. Although they are all connected to the mains, tap water is still a rarity in many villages. In the country many people make a living from their vegetable gardens and by raising a few cows and sheep. The Romanian countryside often looks charming and picturesque, but there is a lot of poverty.

▶ *A village boy stands outside his parents' small farm in the Romanian countryside.*

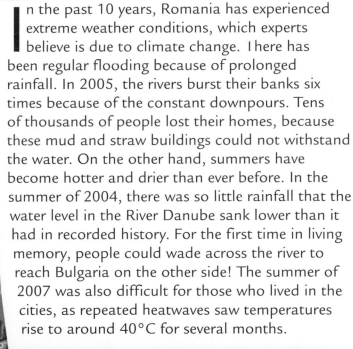

My foal comes everywhere with me!

In the autumn, Ion often goes to the woods with his horse and cart to gather firewood. His wood-burning stove is not only for keeping the house warm but is also used for cooking. The horse has recently given birth to a foal, and Ion takes the young horse everywhere with him. One day the foal will take over the mare's chores – unless Ion has enough money to buy a tractor or truck instead.

Climate

Romania has a temperate continental climate, in which the four seasons are clearly defined. However, in recent years spring has been so warm it seems winter just moves on to summer without any spring at all. The average temperature in winter is -3°C and in summer it is 24°C. There are noticeable differences in the weather across the country. The eastern province of Moldavia is influenced by the extreme Russian climate, and the winters are colder and the summers hotter there. In contrast, the Banat, in the extreme west of the country, enjoys a Mediterranean climate.

▼ *Sibiu in winter, with the Carpathians in the background.*

In the past 10 years, Romania has experienced extreme weather conditions, which experts believe is due to climate change. There has been regular flooding because of prolonged rainfall. In 2005, the rivers burst their banks six times because of the constant downpours. Tens of thousands of people lost their homes, because these mud and straw buildings could not withstand the water. On the other hand, summers have become hotter and drier than ever before. In the summer of 2004, there was so little rainfall that the water level in the River Danube sank lower than it had in recorded history. For the first time in living memory, people could wade across the river to reach Bulgaria on the other side! The summer of 2007 was also difficult for those who lived in the cities, as repeated heatwaves saw temperatures rise to around 40°C for several months.

Provinces and districts

Romania is divided into 40 districts (*judete*) plus the capital Bucharest. The needs of such a large number of districts can be difficult to coordinate, so eight development regions have been formed. Within a region, local authorities work together to use the money for development in a way that benefits everyone.

Moving livestock in a seasonal cycle used to be commonplace in all mountainous areas of Europe. Nowadays, Romania is one of the few countries where this still takes place. The moving of sheep is called *transhumanta* in Romanian (transhumance in English). At the beginning of autumn, the shepherds gather on the high mountain slopes of the Carpathians. They then set off with their flocks of sheep for the plains around the River Danube, where they will spend the winter months.

Around Easter time, when the snow has melted, they return to higher regions. Lambs are then slaughtered for the Easter meal. There are several traditions linked to transhumance, including 'measuring the milk', which was carried out to discover how much cheese the owners of the sheep were entitled to.

There are also the three historical provinces that joined together to become Romania in the twentieth century. Between the Carpathians and the Danube lies Wallachia (called *Tara Româneasca* in Romanian – literally 'the Romanian country'). To the east of the mountains lies Moldavia (*Moldova* in Romanian). The eastern part of historic Moldavia, called Bessarabia, has been annexed by Russia and the Soviet Union throughout history, and since 1991 this has been the independent Republic of Moldavia. Transylvania (*Ardeal* or *Transilvania*) lies to the north and west of the Carpathians.

Rivers and sea

The Danube (*Duanrea* in Romanian) is the second longest river in Europe (after the Volga) and rises in the Black Forest in Germany.

From the forests of the Carpathians, rivers such as the Jiu, the Olt and the Prahova flow downwards through the mountains until they reach the Danube. The Danube splits into three tributaries at the town of Tulcea before gushing into the Black Sea.

The Black Sea coast has broad beaches along which many seaside resorts can be found. The most famous of these is Mamaia, just north of the town of Constanta.

▼ *The Danube squeezes its way towards the Black Sea through a spectacular gap in the Carpathians known as the Iron Gate Gorge.*

◀ *Houses in Sebeş.*

Flag

The Romanian flag has three vertical stripes: blue, yellow and red. During the communist era, the state coat of arms was emblazoned on the middle bar, but this was removed during the revolution. A new coat of arms has been designed but this is no longer part of the flag.

Money

The Romanian currency is the *leu* (plural *lei*), which is divided into 100 *bani*. *Leu* means 'lion' and probably comes from the Dutch 'lion thaler', a coin used in Romania during the seventeenth and eighteenth centuries. The word dollar also comes from the Dutch *thaler*, which was pronounced *daler* in Dutch. The English adopted this form and eventually changed the spelling to dollar. In 2005, four zeros were scrapped from the Romanian *leu* so one new *leu* was worth as much as 10,000 old *lei*. The new notes have been designed so they are as big as euro banknotes. Romania is planning to switch to the euro in 2012–14. Romanian banknotes are made of polymer, a kind of plastic.

▲ *The concert hall of the Romanian Athenaeum in Bucharest is shown on the back of the 5-lei banknote.*

National anthem

After the revolution of 1989, Romania adopted a new national anthem: 'Awaken thee, Romanian!' (see panel). This is a song dating from the nineteenth century that was banned during the communist era because it contains an appeal to revolt against tyrants. It became the anthem for the revolution and was chosen by the people afterwards as the new national anthem.

'Awaken thee, Romanian, shake off the deadly slumber/ The scourge of barbarian tyrannies / And now or never to a bright horizon clamber / That shall to shame put all your enemies.'

◀ *Washing hangs outside a rural house.*

Cities

Just over half the population of Romania live in cities. Many cities have drab apartment blocks built during the communist era, but there are also many lovely old buildings, including castles, churches and houses.

▲ These children say they prefer the countryside to the cities.

Bucharest

Almost two million people live in the capital Bucharest (in Romanian, *Bucuresti*). According to legend, the city takes its name from a shepherd called Bucur who founded it. However, it is more likely that Bucharest was founded in the fourteenth century by merchants. In 1659, Bucharest became the capital of Wallachia and in 1862, the capital of Romania. Before the Second World War Bucharest was nicknamed 'Little Paris' or the 'Paris of the East' because many buildings in the city were built by French architects and because, like Paris, it had a flourishing cultural and artistic life.

Bucharest is situated on the River Dâmbovita, which has been completely converted into a canal where it runs through Bucharest; it disappears underground in the city centre.

▲ The fountains in the centre of Bucharest are lovely and cool in summer.

On the north side of the city there are many small lakes surrounded by parkland. The most famous of these is the Cismigiu garden, which dates from the nineteenth century. This is a beautifully laid-out park with a lot of ponds, statues and outdoor cafés. It can be a haven of peace in the busy city centre.

▼ In the Cismigiu Park in Bucharest, there is a special corner for chess enthusiasts, who can always find an opponent to play against them.

There is a lot of construction work going on in Bucharest, but it is possible to escape to one of the city's many parks. The largest park is Herestrau, just north of the city centre. This contains a large lake, which is good for boating, and nearby is the Village Museum, which has replica farmhouses, windmills, village schools and wooden churches. The park is a good place to walk, jog or roller skate, or to spend a couple of lazy hours in an outdoor café.

It's great to be out in the fresh air!

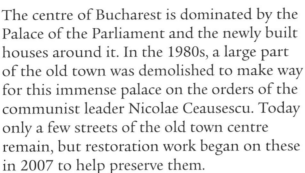

'The street where I chased after Ana'.

The centre of Bucharest is dominated by the Palace of the Parliament and the newly built houses around it. In the 1980s, a large part of the old town was demolished to make way for this immense palace on the orders of the communist leader Nicolae Ceausescu. Today only a few streets of the old town centre remain, but restoration work began on these in 2007 to help preserve them.

▲ Renovation work is ongoing in the old centre of Bucharest.

Bucharest is situated in an earthquake zone, and in 1940 and 1977, earthquakes destroyed part of the city centre. Measuring 7.2 on the Richter scale, the earthquakes were also responsible for the deaths of more than 1,500 people. The climate of the city is not always pleasant, as winters can be very cold and summers terribly hot.

Bucharest is the political, cultural and economic heart of Romania, and is a hive of activity as a result. New buildings are going up in the centre as well as in the suburbs. At the same time, Bucharest is an interesting and dynamic city that attracts many Romanians. The best jobs are found here, but so is a lively lifestyle, with a great deal of culture and entertainment.

▶ Musicians play for money in the Bucharest underground rail system.

Iași

Iași is the second largest city in Romania, with around 400,000 inhabitants. It lies on the River Bahlui and is nicknamed 'the town of the seven hills', like Rome and Istanbul. Iași is mentioned in official records for the first time in 1408. However, there are buildings in the city that are older than this, so it certainly existed before the fifteenth century. In 1640, the first school in which Romanian was taught was established here. Iași was the capital of Moldavia between 1565 and 1862. After the unification of Wallachia and Moldavia in 1862, Bucharest became the only capital of Romania and Iași lost its status. At the end of the nineteenth century the city was modernised, and several beautiful buildings were constructed, including the Palace of Culture, the National Theatre 'Vasile Alecsandri' and the Alexandru Ioan Cuza University.

Cluj

Cluj is the historic capital of Transylvania. The town is also known by its Hungarian name of Kolozsvár and its German name Klausenburg, and has been known in Romania as Cluj-Napoca since 1974. The old Latin name of the city was added to emphasise the fact that the Romans lived in the area 2,000 years ago. Until the First World War, the whole of Transylvania, and thus Cluj, belonged to Austria-Hungary, and most of the people who lived there were Hungarians. Now around 20 per cent of the inhabitants are Hungarian, and there is a Hungarian opera and a Hungarian theatre. Romanian, Hungarian, German and English are all taught at the Babes-Bolyai University, which is the largest university in the country.

▲ *A dog is sold at a market place.*

From 1992 to 2004, Cluj had a nationalistic mayor, Gheorghe Funar, who had all the benches in the city painted in the colours of the Romanian flag. He did this to emphasise the Romanian character of this multicultural city.

◄ *There are trolley buses in many Romanian cities.*

Timişoara is the city where, on 16 December 1989, the revolution heralded the end of the communist era in Romania. When the authorities wanted to forcefully transfer the ethnic Hungarian clergyman László Tökés to another town, a rebellion broke out. In days that followed, this grew into a major uprising against the dictatorship. The army and the security forces fired at the demonstrators and many people were killed, mostly students. On 20 December 1989, Timişoara declared itself to be the first non-communist town in Romania. The revolution in Bucharest had not yet started, but a total of 1,100 people eventually died as the Romanian Revolution swept the country.

▲ On 20 December 1989, communism was overthrown. Behind this street sign stands the Orthodox cathedral of Timişoara.

Timişoara

Timişoara is the capital of the western region known as Banat. The city takes its name from the river Timiş, which flows through it. The Bega canal that lies partly in Romania and partly in Serbia also flows through Timişoara. The canal was dug in the eighteenth century but it has now silted up and has not been navigable since 1956, although there are plans to dig it out again.

In 1855, Timişoara was the first town in the Habsburg Empire to have electricity and in 1884, the first European city with electric street lights. Timişoara is a laid-back city with 14,500 historic monuments – more than any other Romanian town or city. Romanians, Hungarians, Germans and Serbians all live together in Timişoara, although ethnic Romanians make up the majority of the population. This is the only European city with three national theatres; one Romanian, one Hungarian and one German.

Timişoara has experienced an economic boom since the mid-1990s, largely due to foreign investors who have built businesses and factories. Timişoara is also a centre of education and is the most important university city in Romania after Bucharest. Young people from all parts of Romania – and increasingly from other EU countries – go to Timişoara to study. There are plenty of places to visit, including several famous jazz cafés, and from April onwards, the outdoor cafés in the restored city centre are overflowing with people.

◄ A game of football in Timişoara.

Constanţa

The city of Constanţa lies on the Black Sea. This is the most important port in Romania, as well as one of the most popular beach resorts on the Black Sea coast. Where the city now lies there once was a Greek colony called Tomis, and it was to here that Emperor Augustus banished the Greek poet Ovid. There is a statue of Ovid in the central square of Constanţa, where the Archaeological Museum and a beautifully preserved mosaic can also be found. Constanţa is home to the largest mosque in Romania, built between 1910 and 1912. It was the first structure made from reinforced concrete. The area between the Danube and the Black Sea, where Constanţa is situated, has only been part of Romania since 1878; before this it was part of the Ottoman Empire and there are still Turkish and Tartar minorities living in the city.

Other cities

Craiova is the capital of the southern region Oltenia. It is an industrial centre where cars, engines and machines are manufactured, as well as many other products.

Piteşti is a slightly smaller city (190,000 inhabitants). Since 1966, a factory here has built cars with the brand name Dacia, which is now owned by the French company Renault. Piteşti is also known as the 'city of tulips', and a tulip festival takes place here every year. The tulip is originally a Turkish flower and the Romanian name for the flower, *lalea*, is derived from the Turkish *lále*.

▼ *The Constanţa casino in winter.*

Braşov (320,000 inhabitants) was originally a German city called Kronstadt. It is now an important industrial town, with tractor and lorry factories. It is also a good base for winter sport. The ski resort Poina Braşov is only 11 km away. Braşov's most famous building is the fourteenth-century Black Church, which got its name in 1689 after it was completely burnt black by a fire.

Ploieşti (135,000 inhabitants) is the centre of the Romanian oil industry.

Sibiu (160,000 inhabitants) is a flourishing cultural and economic centre in the south of Transylvania, from where the peaks of the Carpathian Mountains can be seen. Sibiu was founded in the twelfth century by German colonists, who gave it the name Hermannstadt. Sibiu was the capital of Transylvania in the eighteenth and nineteenth centuries.

The palace of Baron Samuel von Brukenthal was built in Sibiu between 1778 and 1788, and the baron specified in his will that the palace should be turned into a museum. It became the first museum in Romania. Before the Second World War, the majority of Sibiu's population was ethnic German; now there are fewer than 6,000 Germans here, although the mayor, Klaus Johannis, is a German. In 2007, Sibiu was the first Romanian city to be named European Cultural Capital.

▶ *The village of Cristian (in the district of Sibiu) has a fortified church.*

◄ Sheep in northern Romania.

Transport

Roads in Romania are often poor. There are hardly any motorways, which means that traffic passes through towns and villages.

▲ *Roads in rural areas are often little more than mud tracks.*

As the volume of traffic in Romania is increasing rapidly, motorist and lorry drivers have found driving more and more difficult and dangerous. Many people drive recklessly, and this causes many accidents. Because there are few motorways, people are forced to drive on smaller, two-lane roads, often through rural areas.

New motorways

Before the fall of communism, there were only 100 km of motorways in Romania, running from Bucharest to Piteşti. Since then work has begin on the 'Sun's Motorway' from Bucharest to the Black Sea. The 'Autostrada Transylvania' is also being built. This goes from the Hungarian border to the city of Braşov, where it will eventually be linked to the new A1 to Bucharest. The network of provincial roads is also being repaired, and ring roads are being built around Bucharest. There is still a lot of work to be done in rural areas, though, as only the main road through a village is properly laid. The backstreets are dirt roads, and when it rains they are almost impossible to drive on.

Traffic

Although the Romanian government is working hard to make the roads better, the improvements cannot keep pace with the rise in the amount of traffic. Since 1989, car ownership has risen by 10 per cent every year, resulting in severe traffic problems in many cities. On most days the traffic in Bucharest almost grinds to a halt, and it is often quicker to walk somewhere than drive. However, it can be difficult and dangerous for pedestrians, who have to weave in and out of cars parked on the pavements because there are not enough parking places.

▶ *In Bucharest, the parking problem is so severe that people park on the pavement.*

If I'm quick I'll just make it...

Since 1979 Bucharest has had an underground rail system, which is now being expanded. Above ground, there are buses, trams and trolley buses. Not many people cycle in the cities, although this is a popular form of transport in the country.

▲ *An underground ticket.*

▲ *Many Romanian cities have trolley buses.*

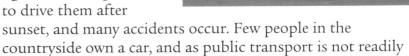

Horses and carts are often used to transport people as well as goods in rural areas. There are believed to be around 750,000 horse-drawn carts still in use in Romania. As they usually do not have lights, it is dangerous to drive them after sunset, and many accidents occur. Few people in the countryside own a car, and as public transport is not readily available, children often have to walk a long way to school. Not all villages have secondary schools so children have to go to boarding school or board with families in the city if they want to keep studying.

◄ *It is not uncommon in Romania to see people travelling by horse and cart, particularly in the countryside.*

▶ *Ferry across the Danube.*

Shipping

The Danube is the only river in Romania navigable by large boats. Most sea-going vessels on their way to the Black Sea avoid the Danube delta and travel instead via the Danube-Black Sea Canal. Building began on this canal in the 1950s, and it was notorious because the work was carried out by forced labour gangs – prisoners who had opposed the communist regime. Work stopped in 1955 and not resumed until 1975. The work was finished in 1984 and cost around £1 billion.

The port of Constanţa is one of the 10 largest in Europe. It is a major transit port between countries in the middle and eastern parts of Europe and Central Asia and the Middle East. There has been a port here since the sixth century BC, but the first stone of the present-day port was laid in 1896 by King Carol I. Since then, the port has constantly been modernised and expanded. The latest developments are the construction of a container terminal in 2004 and a passenger terminal in 2005.

Railways

▲ *At the station in Piteşti, the 'Blue Arrow' sets off for Bucharest.*

The Romanian Rail Company (*Căile Ferate Române*, or CFR) has a dense network of railway lines totalling 14,484 km. Ten per cent of the rail company is owned by private companies. CFR has been modernising the railways since 2000: new locomotives and carriages have been bought and many stations have been renovated. Many of the trains have sleeping carriages – if you take the sleeper at 11 p.m. from Bucureşti-Nord (Bucharest-North) to Iaşi, you can sleep for the whole journey and arrive rested at 5.40 the following morning. The longest train journey in Romania, from Suceava in the north-east to Timişoara in the west, takes 15 hours.

Aviation

Although there are airports in 15 Romanian cities, domestic flights have not replaced transport by car, train or bus because it is still quite expensive to fly. The most important international airport is Henri Coandă in the village of Otopeni to the north of Bucharest. Timişoara, Cluj, Constanţa and Sibiu also have international airports.

The national airline company, TAROM (*Transporturile Aeriene Române*, Romanian Air Transport), flies to many destinations in Europe and the Middle East. British Airways also now flies 10 times a week from Bucharest to London and back.

◀ *The national airline, TAROM, flies throughout Europe.*

People

Throughout its history, many different peoples have lived in the area that is now Romania. There are still several ethnic minorities, although most of the population are ethnic Romanians.

▲ *Selling lottery tickets on the street.*

Population groups

In 2002, a census was carried out, which revealed the ethnic distribution of the people of Romania. Ninety per cent of the population are ethnic Romanians, although some consider themselves to be Moldavian. There is a Romanian minority in North Bucovina, an area that now belongs to the Ukraine. There are also Romanian minorities in Serbia and Hungary.

The largest minority in Romania is made up of 1.4 million Hungarians – 6.6 per cent of the population. In the Transylvanian provinces of Harghita and Covasna they are actually in the majority. Relations between Romanians and Hungarians have not always been easy but today they are quite good. Hungarian is considered an official language in a city if at least 20 per cent of the population speak it. Hungarians celebrate their national day on 15 March, even in Romania; they will display the Hungarian flag, put on their national costume and hold processions and parades.

▲ *The daily paper* Libertatea *is the most popular newspaper in Romania.*

◄ *Not everyone has a mobile phone, so public payphones can still be seen all over Romania.*

▶ A Roma family collects wood in the forest.

Roma

The Roma (or gypsies) are the third largest population group, at 2.5 per cent of the total. In fact there are probably more Roma than this (possibly up to 10 per cent), but many Roma claimed to be Romanian or Hungarian when the census was taken, depending on which language they spoke.

Many Roma live in severe poverty in huts in the countryside or in dingy flats in run-down city neighbourhoods. The life expectancy of the Roma is 15 years less than that of the other population groups. The government has initiated several programmes to improve the situation of the Roma but it is a difficult task. The Roma keep to their own traditions and customs, and reject the culture of the *gadjes* (the non-Roma). They can find it hard to get work because there is a great deal of discrimination against them.

◀ Some Roma travel in covered wagons for part of the year.

Some Roma have found success in the music business – gypsy music is very poplar in Romania and the Roma can earn a lot by performing their music and selling CDs. The band *Taraf de Haidouks* ('Band of Gypsies') is particularly popular.

Germans

There used to be many Germans in Romania, especially in Transylvania, where they settled originally in the twelfth century. They were known as Saxons, although they came not only from Saxony but also from the south of the Netherlands. Near the town of Alba Iulia, for example, there is a village called Bărăbanţ which is clearly derived from Brabant, a southern Dutch province. In the eighteenth century, Germans also settled in the western region of Banat. There they are known as Schwaben.

In 1930, there were still 800,000 ethnic Germans living in Romania, but most of these emigrated and now the German population is around 60,000.

◀ Billboards cover the fronts of apartment blocks.

▶ *A house in Şieu.*

Other minorities include the Turks and Tartars (55,000). They live mainly in the area between the Danube and the Black Sea. Before the Second World War, there were many Jews in Romania but many were killed in the war, and others fled to Israel and the USA because of persecution. Now there are fewer than 6,000 Jews in Romania.

Religion

Romanians are very religious. During the last census only 20,000 (0.1 per cent of the population) said they did not believe in God. Almost all ethnic Romanians belong to the Romanian Orthodox Church. As Orthodox believers, they have the same religion as, for example, the Greeks, the Bulgarians and the Russians. The Romanians see their religion as an essential part of their national identity. They are the only Latin people who are not Catholic but Orthodox.

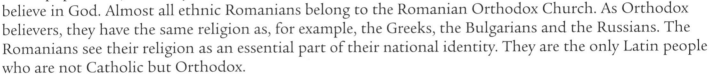

The Hungarians and Germans in the country are usually Catholic or Protestant. There are also ethnic Romanians who belong to new Protestant churches such as the Adventist or the Pentecostal churches.

◀ *In 'the merry cemetery' in Săpânţa (in the district of Maramureş), the crosses are decorated and include poems.*

Most Romanians have at least one first name that is derived from the name of a saint, and Romanians celebrate a 'birthday' on their saints day. For example, 6 December is the saints day for Saint Nicolas (in Romanian *Sfântul-Niclae*), and everybody with the name Niculae, Nicolae or Nicu celebrates this, as well as those with female derivatives of the name, such as Nicole and Nicoletta. On 7 January, the name day of *Sfântul-Ioan* (Saint John or John the Baptist), almost two million Romanians with the name Ion, Ioan, Iona, Ionel or Ionuţ celebrate their name day.

Posters and fliers have been pasted everywhere in the centre of Bucharest to advertise an intensive yoga course. All other posters with concert announcements are constantly covered by these posters, which claim that people can change their lives through yoga!

The communist regime was officially atheistic – that is, people were discouraged from practising a religion. However, there was no law to say that people couldn't go to church. Since the fall of communism, Romania has experienced a religious revival. On religious holidays in particular, the churches are full. Many young people choose a life as a monk or a nun in one of the many monasteries and convents in Romania. On 14 October, Saint Paraschiva's day, at least a million Romanians make a pilgrimage to the town of Iaşi, where the relics of the saint have been kept since 1641.

Decreasing population

The Romanian population is decreasing – Romanian families are traditionally small, and many people left the country in search of a better life after the fall of communism. In 2000, there were 22.3 million Romanians; by 2007, this had dropped to 21.5 million and it is expected that there will only be 16.8 million by 2050. As the world population is soaring, some people think it is good when populations in certain countries decline, but there is a concern that this will result in an ageing population in countries like Romania in 50 years or so. Many elderly people will be dependent on a generation with fewer young people than ever before.

► *A young girl helps her grandfather to pick apples.*

◀ *Students often help out their parents at the market on weekends to earn a bit of pocket money.*

Romanians place great importance on the family, and it is customary for the elderly to live with their children. They often look after the grandchildren as, in most families, both the mother and the father work and childcare is not very well developed.

When Romania became part of the European Union in 2007, there were about 1.5 million Romanians working abroad. Most of them believe this is only temporary, but there will undoubtedly be many who will not return home because they have settled in their new country, have jobs, and children who go to school and have friends there.

Language

According to the Romanian poet Mihai Eminescu, the beauty of the Romanian language was a sign of the moral superiority of the Romanians. Even so, the Romanians spoke Old Church Slavonic (or Old Bulgarian) as an official language in church and government until the sixteenth century. A letter from 1521 is the oldest surviving document in the Romanian language.

▶ *Mihai Eminescu.*

Romanians are great book lovers, and second-hand books are eagerly snapped up. There are not many Romanian writers who are known abroad, but the Romanians are proud of their national poet Mihai Eminescu (1850–89).

Romanian words

Da	Yes
Nu	No
Bună ziua!	Good day!
Bună seara!	Good evening!
Salut!	Hello
Ce mai faci?	How are you?
Bine	Fine
Noroc!	Cheers!
Mulțumesc	Thank you
La revedere!	Goodbye
Unu, doi, trei...	One, two, three...
Bucureștiul este capitala României	Bucharest is the capital of Romania

Like French, Spanish and Italian, Romanian is directly descended from Latin. However, the language differs in many ways from the other Romance languages in the West. The Romanian vocabulary includes many words derived from other languages, including Slavic, Greek, Turkish, German and Hungarian. From the nineteenth century onwards, when people realised the importance of their Latin heritage, French words were adopted more often. The Romanians used the Cyrillic (Slavonic) alphabet, with a few exceptions, until the nineteenth century. It was then decided to write Romanian in the Latin alphabet. In principle, one character is used for each sound. Romanian also has the letters ș, ț, ă, â and î, pronounced 'sj', 'ts', silent 'e' and the last two sound like 'uh'.

As soon as the weather is good, children play football outside their village Odvoș in the district of Arad. Football is the most popular sport in Romania and the country has produced many famous footballers, such as Gheorge Hagi, Gică Popescu, Christian Chivu and Adrian Mutu.

Real Madrid is my favourite...

Country traditions

In many parts of the Romanian countryside, traditions are practised every day, not just for the benefit of tourists. Potters, woodcutters, icon painters, weavers and embroiderers still ply their trade as their ancestors did.

Romanian folk music is known and appreciated far and wide. Some bands have become famous through playing a mixture of folk and pop music. Although there are some people who dislike this kind of music, it is particularly popular amongst young people – and they like to play it loudly!

◄ Mr and Mrs Sas live in a village in the district of Maramures, where their grandparents and great-grandparents also lived.

Education

The education system in Romania has changed a great deal since the communist era. New subjects have been introduced to the curriculum and new textbooks have been written.

There are many people who do not think this is enough, and who believe that a major education reform is still needed.

▲ *The new school uniform (see page 32).*

Funding

People often complain that not enough money is spent on education in Romania. They believe that run-down school buildings should be renovated and that teachers should be paid more. Many teachers have to take second jobs just to earn enough money to live.

In the communist era, all children belonged to the youth section of the Communist Party. Pupils at secondary schools were 'Pioneers'; primary school children were 'Falcons of the Fatherland'. The Falcons wore orange blouses and a red tie – the symbol of communism.

There are sometimes not enough school buildings in a town or district to cope with the numbers of children in that area. When this happens, some children go to school in the mornings and some in the afternoons. Staying at school during the lunch break is not typical – most have their lunch at home. Romanian children eat a hot meal when they come home.

◄ *This school is in the small town of Sânnicolau-Mare.*

According to a report in 2007, despite the reforms of the past 20 years, Romanian education still falls short of the standards reached in most other European countries.

▶ *School books for sale in the Obor Square in Bucharest.*

▶ *Children at break in a country school.*

The school system

After nursery school, which lasts between one and three years, all children go to primary school at the age of seven. This lasts eight years and is compulsory and free of charge for all Romanian children. School uniform was abolished after the revolution, but has now been reintroduced and is compulsory at all state schools.

Although primary school is compulsory, many children still do not attend all the time, particularly in rural areas. Farmer's children often have to stay home and help on the farm and not all Roma send their children to school, as they have not had any education themselves, so they do not consider it particularly important.

In some village schools there are four rather than eight classes and some children have to go to a nearby, larger village that does have a school with eight classes. Public transport is not always available and this means that they have to walk several kilometres there and back again. This is not always possible, so some children miss out even on their primary education.

◀ *Romanian school uniforms have a pupil number and the name of the school on the sleeve.*

At school there is whole-class teaching, children have to learn a lot by heart and there is not much time for creative subjects. They regularly go on school trips, but these are usually educational outings, such as a visit to a museum or a monument.

One of these young football fans supports Dinamo Bucharest and the other Steaua Bucharest, but they are still best friends. After school they love to play football on the patch of grass between the apartment blocks. The only thing they worry about is the ball ending up in the road.

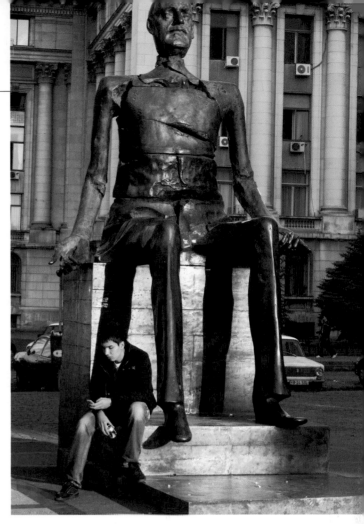

▶ A young man waits for his friends after school.

At the end of primary school, all children take a proficiency exam in Romanian language and literature, maths, history and geography. They must pass this exam if they are to continue their education at secondary level.

In 2007, the issue of compulsory religious education came up for discussion. All recognised religions in Romania had asked for this. Religious education was was already taught at most schools, but there was no law to make it compulsory. Children who did not want to follow religious education or whose parents disagreed with it, studied religious history instead. In the end, the law was not passed and religious study continues in the same way.

In the days of communism, a portrait of President Nicolae Ceausescu hung in every classroom. After the revolution, these were removed and usually replaced by icons, often with a picture of Mary with the baby Jesus. In 2006, a teacher demanded that all those icons and other religious symbols on the walls be forbidden as it was discrimination against unbelievers and followers of other religions. For months a fight went on in the media between supporters and opponents of icons in schools. In the summer of 2007, the Court of Appeal ruled that religious symbols could only be hung up during religious education. However, that does not mean that all icons were immediately taken off the walls.

Secondary school has four classes (five for students taking evening classes). At the end of secondary school, children must take final exams, which are made up of five tests: three written and two oral. The written and oral tests in Romanian language and literature are compulsory. The other three subjects are selected by the students themselves.

Passing these final exams means students can apply to study at university or vocational college. However, they must pass an entrance exam before they are accepted.

For a number of subjects, such as medicine and information technology, there are more candidates than places, so it it very competitive. To have a better chance of succeeding, students sometimes take a year off to prepare for the entrance examination.

▶ Students preparing for a study group.

For the last few years, higher education in Romania has followed a bachelor-master system similar to that found in the UK or USA. It takes two or three years to study for a bachelor's degree. Particularly academic students might choose to study for a further two years to obtain a master's degree. After that the whizz-kids can do doctoral research to gain a PhD.

Private schools

As well as state schools, there are also private schools and universities in Romania. If pupils cannot get into a state school, there is the option of going to a private school, but school fees are high and not many people can afford them. There is also a system of scholarships, but only the best students are eligible for these.

Native language education

In principle, every child has the right to be educated in their native language, but in practice this is only possible for children who belong to one of the larger ethnic-minority groups. Hungarian children, for example, can be educated from nursery level to university in their own language. A few years ago, education in Romanes, the language of the Roma, was introduced to primary schools, but this move was controversial because some people argued that Roma children would never learn Romanian. Without being able to speak the national language they would find it even more difficult to find a job after they finished their education.

▶ *Most students try to earn a little extra money. This young woman helps her parents by working in their shop at the weekend.*

Cuisine

Romanians are great meat eaters. There is a saying that the tastiest vegetable is a piece of meat! They do eat a lot of salads, but cooked vegetables as a side dish are not very popular.

Romanian cuisine is similar to that of other countries on the Balkan Peninsula, such as Bulgaria and Serbia, but has been influenced by mid-European cuisine, such as that of Hungary.

▲ *During the Cow Parade in 2005, painted cows could be seen everywhere in Bucharest.*

Home-grown food

Supermarkets are becoming increasingly popular, but traditionally Romanians buy many food items at the market, where farmers sell home-grown produce. Since Romania joined the EU, however, many farmers can no longer sell at the market because they are unable to produce the food in surroundings that are hygienic enough to meet the strict EU regulations.

▲ *The European Union no longer allows milk to be sold at the market or in the street.*

Many people in the countryside still live on what they can grow on their small farms or in their gardens. They might keep a cow and a few chickens, and grow cabbages, tomatoes, cucumbers and sweet peppers in their vegetable gardens.

▶ *A small shop.*

My herbs will improve the flavour of any dish!

This woman has been selling herbs at the market in Craiova for years. It hasn't made her rich, but every little helps! She likes working on her market stall, as she can enjoy a chat with other women from her village.

National dishes

Romania has two national dishes: the favourite meat dish is *mici* or *mititei*, which literally means 'little ones'. These are spicy meat rolls, lightened by the use of baking soda. They are tastiest when grilled and eaten with mustard.

▲ *Sarmale with mămăliă.*

Real winter fare includes *sarmale* (minced meat in cabbage leaves or grape leaves with sauerkraut and bacon), which should be eaten with *mămălia* (a sort of corn porridge). These used to be staple foods when bread was a luxury, but bread is now eaten with every meal; the Romanians always eat their hot meal with a few chunks of bread.

Romanians serve food that might be considered unusual in Britain. The most traditional restaurants serve *ciorbă de burtă* (tripe soup), which is made from the stomach of a cow; in many countries, this is offal that is only fed to animals! Calf's brain is also considered a delicacy in Romania, and some restaurants even serve bear meat.

▶ *Romanian restaurants in other countries, such as the Netherlands, serve the Romanian speciality tripe soup.*

What can you have to eat in Romania when you are walking through the city and suddenly feel really hungry? How about a spicy roll with meat or cheese? *Covrigi*, a kind of large pretzel with sesame seeds, are delicious, but if you prefer something sweet, you can buy apple tart or *gogoşi*, a kind of doughnut ball with raisins or currants. In autumn you can sometimes buy sweet chestnuts in paper cornets, or bags of grilled corncobs. But the fast food industry has also arrived, so you can satisfy your hunger with a hamburger or a kebab just like you can in countries all over the world.

▲ *Romanians are great cheese lovers.*

Slaughtering and fasting

In the country, it is traditional to slaughter a pig a few days before Christmas. Animals are fattened throughout the year especially so they can be part of the Christmas feast. Because of strict EU rules recently introduced, animals are no longer allowed to just be slaughtered in the garden as they once were. Pigs have to be inspected by a vet and made into chops and sausages in hygienic surroundings. At Easter time, the Romanians traditionally eat lamb.

◄ *Everyone is looking forward to the festive meal.*

Many Orthodox Christian Romanians fast at various times of the year, which means that they will not eat certain kinds of food, especially meat, but also cheese and eggs. The periods of fasting include the seven weeks before Easter called the Great Fast or Lent, and the 40 days of the Christmas Fast. Exceptions are made for certain days during that period, when they are allowed to eat fish.

During the fasting periods, people are not allowed to get married, as weddings are always accompanied by huge festive meals that last for several days.

▶ *A fish restaurant in the Olt valley.*

Eating well in Romania means eating a lot, so a guest at the table, especially a foreign guest, will usually be pressured into eating too much from the food-laden table!

> They never sting me ... well, almost never.

The beekeeper from the village of Sieu, in the far north of Romania, receives financial aid from the government to make natural honey. The bees feed on the acacia trees in the middle of the countryside, where there are no factories and almost no traffic. However, the beekeeper finds it hard to make a living selling his jars of honey in the European market because it is difficult to compete.

Drink

The national drink is *țuică* (pronounced 'tsoejkeh') or *palincă* (twice-distilled *țuică*). It is usually made from plums, but can also be made from other fruit or from pomace – the residue that remains after pressing grapes. The EU is planning to impose restraints on the brewing of strong liquor, but people in the countryside will probably continue to make their traditional drink.

People have grown grapes to make wine in Romania since Roman times, but the industry was neglected during the communist era. Since the 1990s, however, Romanian vineyards have been producing excellent wines again. The climate and the good soil are ideal for growing grapes.

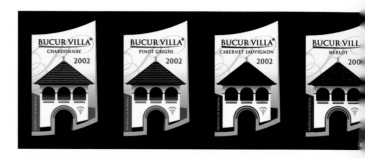

▲ *Romanian red wine from various types of grapes.*

Romanians are real coffee drinkers and will spend hours over a cup of coffee and a chat. The traditional Turkish coffee served throughout the Balkans is losing ground to cappuccino, espresso and other types that have been introduced from the West.

◄ *According to the label, this wine from Recaș gives you strength.*

Recipe for *Mititei*

Ingredients
1 kg minced beef or 1 kg beef and pork mince, pepper, cumin, baking soda, stock, salt, garlic.

Mix a pinch of pepper, a dash of cumin, a teaspoon of baking soda and salt (to taste) together with the minced meat. If you like spicy food, mix in a teaspoon of hot paprika. Crush a generous amount of garlic cloves together with a dash of stock. Do this in the traditional way, with a mortar and pestle. Mix this into the mince and put it in the fridge for a couple of hours. If it is too dry, add a little stock. Make small rolls about 5 cm long from this mixture. They can then be fried or grilled. Keep them moist by brushing them with stock. The Romanians prefer them slightly raw, but you can fry or grill them for as long as you want. Serve with strong mustard and use a cocktail stick to eat them.

Economy

The Romanians have a saying that they live in a rich country with poor inhabitants.

Romania has fertile soil, a good climate, many mineral reserves, the Danube and the Black Sea for water supplies, and a good location at the crossroads of trade routes between north and south. Yet, because of the country's turbulent history, the population has not always been able to profit from this.

▲ *Hay is transported from the fields by ox-cart.*

Farming

Romania is traditionally an agricultural country and other industries developed late here compared to other European countries. Until the nineteenth century, 90 per cent of the population lived in villages and worked on the land. As farmers usually worked for a landowner or only had a small patch of land, they often lived in great poverty.

Industrial development began towards the end of the nineteenth century, and in the period between the two world wars, Romania's economy grew rapidly. During this period, after the territory had been expanded to include Transylvania and Bessarabia, the rural population dropped to 80 per cent.

When the communists came to power after the Second World War, all companies, factories and shops were nationalised, which meant they were in the hands of the state rather than privately owned. The communist rulers wanted to industrialise the country quickly, which they believed would improve the economy. Farmers were forced to become nothing more than labourers, and made to give up their land to collective farms owned and run by the state.

▼ *The fields are ready for sowing. The Carpathians can be seen in the background.*

▶ *If you don't own any land, your horses have to graze along the roadside.*

By the time the communist regime collapsed, Romania was long overdue an economic overhaul. For example, aircraft, lorries, cars and oil tankers were all manufactured in Romania, but they were of such poor quality that they could not compete with those produced in Western factories, which had more workers and better equipment.

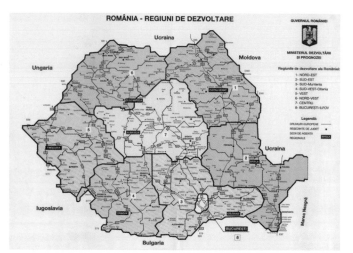

◀ *The eight development regions of Romania.*

Privatisation and investment

In 1990, the new democratic government faced the difficult task of improving Romania's economy and infrastructure so that it could compete on the international market. A market economy like that in the West – driven by supply and demand – had to replace the state-owned regime. Private companies were once more permitted and state companies were sold to private buyers or to companies, often from other countries.

One result of these reforms was that many big companies had close down or sack large numbers of people. However, some people benefited from the changes and became very rich.

After a number of years of decline, the Romanian economy began to grow again in 2000. In 2004, the economic growth rate had reached 8.2 per cent and it has continued steadily since then. This is in large part due to foreign investement, as foreign-owned companies established factories in Romania. The UK exports goods to Romania and is also one of the leading foreign investors.

Romania's rapid economic development over the past 10 years has resulted in a society where many people work extremely hard. There are not enough qualified IT workers, accountants and managers, for example, so there are not enough employees to do the work. In 2007, there was a scandal when a 29-year-old woman was found dead in her apartment. The cause of death was established as exhaustion – she had been working constantly for months, without a break even for Christmas and New Year. This case is not unique in Romania, because having a career and earning a decent living means putting work above all else, even health and family.

▼ *Romania has a flourishing film industry. Some films have won international prizes.*

Foreign investors are attracted to Romania because employees are usually very well trained and labour costs are low compared to those in Western Europe, which means that a company that establishes itself in Romania spends less money on employees. There are now many contracting firms in Romania – for example, textiles are imported, clothes are made in Romania, then they are exported again to countries all over the world.

Subsidies

The European Union has granted Romania substantial subsidies to help develop the country's society and infrastructures such as the road network and public transport. Even while Romania was still under consideration for membership of the EU it received hundreds of millions of euros a year.

Around 30 billion euros have been allocated to Romania from the EU for the period 2007–12. Sixty per cent of this amount is intended to develop the agriculture industry and rural parts of the country.

◀ *Fruit trees are sold at a market in spring.*

Mihai plays his accordion while sitting on a wall in the centre of Bucharest. He keeps on smiling but he does not really feel cheerful. He only receives a tiny pension – hardly enough to live on – so he has to play his music to earn a little extra.

Earning a living

Most people earn very little and there are hardly any unemployment benefits. This has forced many Romanians to seek better conditions in other countries, especially Spain and Italy. Since 2001, Romanians have not needed a visa to travel to countries in the European Union.

It is estimated that between 1.5 and two million Romanians work in other countries. They send a lot of money home, but people who work abroad find it difficult if their children have to stay behind with family or friends in Romania. Sometimes children feel abandoned by their parents and miss them terribly. Yet many Romanians feel they have little choice but to work abroad because of the higher pay – they hope to build a better future for their children. The number of Romanian migrant workers is so high that there are not enough workers left in the country, especially in the building and healthcare industries. Foreign workers from neighbouring countries, such as Moldavia and the Ukraine, as well as from countries such as Pakistan, Bangladesh and China, are employed in Romania in their place.

▶ *Home-made kitchen utensils.*

Romania has an ancient tradition of folk art. Folk dancing and folk music as well as traditional handicrafts are still very much alive. Men may make pottery or work as carpenters, while women do needlework, knitting, crochet and weaving. They then sell their pottery, wooden objects, carpets, tablecloths and small rugs in local markets. Farmers usually try to sell their wares in places that attract a lot of Romanian and foreign tourists. The money that they earn from this is a welcome extra.

Towards larger farms

Twenty per cent of the Romanian population still lives in rural areas, and traditional farming methods – where work is done by hand on small plots of land – is still widespread. However, membership of the European Union is likely to result in changes in this area. Larger, mechanised farms will probably become more common, where work is carried out by machinery such as combine harvesters. The area around the Danube has the most fertile soil and is already the main agricultural region, especially for growing maize and wheat. Products such as soya and rape seed are gaining more ground.

Industry

Romania once had quite large reserves of oil, but most of these have now been used up, although new oil wells have been struck in the Black Sea. The country does have an extensive petrochemical industry, but the oil for this is imported. The most important Romanian products are textiles and shoes, machines and vehicles, metal and metal products, minerals and fuel. Most trade in Romania takes place with other countries in the European Union.

Tourism

Romania's unspoilt countryside, charming old towns, picturesque villages, rugged mountain landscapes and the sandy beaches of the Black Sea coast make it an ideal holiday destination.

Romania is not yet a major tourist hot-spot, but tourism is increasing every year and is an important part of the economy.

Bran Castle towers high above the mountain pass that connects Transylvania with southern Romania. At the end of the fourteenth century the German community that lived in this region built the first incarnation of the castle in the nearby town of Braşov. This has been rebuilt several times in its history, as well as being extended and strengthened several times over the centuries. It is now one of the biggest tourist attractions in Romania, partly because of its beautiful mountain setting. Visitors are told that this is Dracula's castle, but in fact Vlad the Impaler only ever spent one night here. Tourists are advised to hang a string of garlic around their necks, though – just in case...

A growth market

Tourism is a growth market in Romania – the number of foreign visitors has risen since the country became a member of the EU. At the same time, more and more Romanians have started to take holidays within their own country. New hotels and guest houses are springing up everywhere to accommodate the rise in visitor numbers.

Most tourists go to the sea or the mountains. Along the Black Sea coast, there is a string of holiday resorts that cater for those wanting a beach holiday. The Carpathians are a popular destination in both winter as summer, offering opportunities for skiing and hiking.

▼ *The Selses river.*

Romanians are great nature lovers and enjoy travelling into the countryside on Sundays and public holidays to enjoy 'a meal in the green grass' as they call it – a picnic. In the hills and mountains, many country cottages and holiday homes are now being built by wealthier city dwellers, who want to spend their free time away from the busy city.

The royal palace Peleş in Sinia, nicknamed the 'Pearl of the Carpathians'.

The sun and sea tourism along the Black Sea has had a lot of competition from Bulgaria, Hungary, Greece, and more recently, Tunisia. These countries also attract many Romanian tourists.

Holidays on the farm

Romania's tourism potential lies in the development of small-scale individual enterprises that offer tourists the chance to experience the 'real' Romania. It is often possible to stay on a farm, and guest houses with only one or two rooms are increasingly found in popular tourist areas. It is often much nicer to stay in these small, traditional places than in the large hotels.

Folk art is sold at the market in Craiova.

Romanian sun and sea tourism is concentrated on sandy beaches running along the Black Sea that the Romanians call the *litoral*. There are 16 resorts along this riviera, of which Mamaia is the most famous. Costineşti is more popular among young people because it has a livelier night life. Tourists from home and abroad visit the *litoral* for a health cure. The black mud dredged up from the nearby Teirighol Lake is said to have healing properties for skin and bone diseases. Culture lovers can visit the remains of the Greek cities of Histria, Tomis and Callatis, which were established along the coast hundreds of years ago, or admire the Roman mosaic and the archaeological museum of Constanţa.

Another popular attraction for people travelling through Romania by car is Maramureş in the far north. Here, visitors can enjoy the scenery of the Iza valley and admire the eighteenth-century churches and carved gates. From here it is possible to cross the Prislop pass into Moldavia and see the beautifully decorated churches and the stunning scenery in the district of Bucovina.

Frescos adorn the monastery in Sucevita.

▶ *Hunedoara is the largest castle in Romania.*

The town of Sibiu contains several good examples of Central European architecture. There are charming 'German' villages in the lovely rural surroundings of Mărginimea Sibiului, many of which have fortified churches or church fortresses. These churches date from the early Middle Ages, and people sheltered here from marauding Tartars.

Bucharest

Bucharest may be busy, crowded and ugly in parts, but it is also a lively and dynamic city that attracts thousands of visitors every year. 'Ceausescu's Palace', as it is popularly known, can be visited if there is no congress or conference taking place, and tourists are often overwhelmed by the profusion of chandeliers, marble floors and grand reception rooms. It is possible to visit the eighteenth-century Stavropoleos church or have a drink in the wood-timbered *Carul cu Bere* (beer cellar), dating from 1879. The open air Village Museum is also worth visiting. There, you will see examples of traditional houses, windmills and schools as they once could be found in the country.

◀ *Bucharest's beer cellar is one of the oldest drinking establishments.*

Something for everyone

Romania has something to offer visitors whatever season of the year they go there. In fact, summer is not always the best time to visit, as the high temperatures can be unpleasant – unless you are trekking in the mountains, which are cooler. Both spring and autumn are also ideal for a tour through the Carpathians, and in the winter the skiing here is excellent.

Adventurous tourists can enjoy the imposing scenery of the Danube delta. You can take a boat trip through the labyrinth of small waterways and little lakes, which have unique flora and fauna. Staying with local people means waking up and falling asleep to the smell of freshly fried fish. Spoonbills and hundreds of other bird species abound, and with a little luck the visitor might chance upon a colony of pelicans.

Even in Roman times, Romania was known for its mineral springs, and there are several spa towns, which attract people looking for relief from ailments or just a relaxing break. The black mud found along the Black Sea is said to be good for alleviating the symptoms of rheumatism.

▶ *Romania has many mineral springs – some were already being used in Roman times.*

Nature

The three most important geographical features of Romania are the Carpathians, the Danube and the Black Sea. The scenery is varied and often unspoiled, and the Romanian countryside is a haven for nature-lovers.

Mountains and valleys

The Carpathian mountain range curves through Romania for a distance of 909 km from north to west. Four of the peaks here stand higher than 2,438 m. The highest is the Moldoveneanu summit (2,544 m) in the Făgăraş massif.

The lower flanks of the Carpathians are called the sub-Carpathians. These are rolling hills, often covered with dense woods where mainly birch and sessile oak grow. On the hillsides – scattered with haystacks – sheep roam under the watchful eye of shepherds. There are also many fruit trees here.

Rivers and seas

The Danube forms the largest river delta in Europe where it flows into the Black Sea. The Danube delta has been on the UNESCO World Heritage list since 1991; 90 per cent of the area lies in Romania and 10 per cent in the Ukraine. Although the delta is quite large, only 15,000 people live there. The only paved road in the Romanian part is the quay in the little town of Sulina.

The Danube delta forms a labyrinth of waterways and brooks, floating islands and reed lands where more than 1,200 species of plants grow, 300 species of birds nest and 200 kinds of fish can be found (of which the sturgeon is much sought after for its caviar). There are also pelican colonies in the Danube delta, which are found hardly anywhere else in Europe.

▲ *A pelican colony in the Danube delta.*

The Romanian Black Sea is almost 200 km long and, except for the Danube delta, is made up of sandy beaches. Four rivers other than the Danube flow into the Black Sea: the Dnjepr, the Dnjestr, the Don and the Koeban.

▶ *Winter landscape with church and river.*

◀ *Deforestation in the Carpathians.*

According to an old saying, Romanians are the 'brothers of the forest'. It is true that Romanians love their forests and sing their praises in folk poetry and traditional songs. In times past, the country was almost completely covered with forests, but now only about a quarter of Romania is forested. The woods and forests provided good hiding places for people fleeing from invaders or bandits. Sometimes these criminals themselves hid in the woods to avoid being caught. Today, illegal deforestation takes place because there is good money to be had by selling the wood. This is bad for the environment and increases the risk of soil erosion and flooding. In 2003, the government launched a programme of reafforestation, but there is not enough money available yet for this programme to be properly effective and more must be invested to help save Romania's forests.

Nature reserves

Romania has 11 national parks, but these are only accessible to hikers. The oldest is the Tetezat Park, which became a protected area in 1935. Around 900 different species of plant grow here.

In the Carpathians, bears, lynx and wolves live and aurochs (a large type of cattle) can sometimes still be seen. The Romanian bears are so bold that they go into the villages in search of food. Some people have been injured when they didn't get out of a bear's way quickly enough. Bears are hunted on a minor scale, but other rare animals such as the European bison and the aurochs are protected in the nature reserves.

Caves

Hundreds of caves are hidden in the mountains. One of the most famous is the Bear Cave, which earned its name because hundreds of skeletons of cave bears – which became extinct 15,000 years ago – were found here.

Environment

Environmental issues were completely ignored during the communist era, as the government felt that increasing industry was more important than protecting the environment. As a result a great deal of pollution was caused by all the factories. In 1990, Copsa Mica became famous as the 'filthiest town in Europe'. The most polluting factories have been closed down now, but the smelter here is still in use and it will be years before the environment has fully recovered.

As a member of the European Union, Romania must meet the environmental standards set by the organisation. Romanians are becoming more aware of environmental problems, but a truly 'green' way of thinking has yet to evolve.

▶ *The pollution of the town of Copsa Mica can clearly be seen in these computer enhanced aerial photographs. Carbon black used to be made here for blackening car tyres. Although the situation is improving, there is still some way to go in solving Romania's pollution problems.*

Glossary

communism a political system in which all land and property are owned by the state.

Cyrillic alphabet a system of writing based on the Greek alphabet and used in Slavic countries.

democracy a political system in which the people of a country choose who they wish to represent them in government.

dictator a leader who has complete control of a country, without a government.

exiled sent away from a country or region as a punishment.

Middle Ages the period from around AD 500 to 1450.

Orthodox Church the Christian Church in the East; it has several independent sects, including Romanian Orthodox.

petrochemical chemical products made from the raw materials of petroleum or oil.

propaganda information spread to further a particular cause.

subsidies money paid by a government to help businesses that benefit the public.

Index

animals 47
Antonescu, Ion 9
architecture 16, 45
aviation 24
Banat 13, 19, 26
beaches 14, 20, 43, 44, 46
Bessarabia 14, 39
birds 45, 46
Black Sea 12, 14, 20, 22, 24, 27, 39, 42, 43, 44, 45, 46
Brasov 21, 22, 43
Brukenthal, Samuel von 21
Bucharest 10, 12, 14, 16, 17, 18, 19, 22, 23, 24, 28, 41, 45
Bulgaria 8, 12, 13, 35, 44
canals 16, 19, 24
Carol I 8, 24
Carol II 9
Carpathian Mountains 5, 14, 21, 43, 45, 46, 47
Ceausescu, Nicolae 4, 10, 11, 17, 33
climate 13, 17, 38, 39
communism 4, 10, 11, 12, 15, 16, 19, 22, 24, 28, 31, 33, 38, 39, 40, 47
Constanta 14, 20, 24, 44
Craiova 20, 36
currency 15
Cuza, Alexandru Ioan 7, 8, 18
Danube, River 5, 12, 13, 14, 20, 24, 27, 39, 42, 45, 46
Dracula 6, 43
drink 38
economy 9, 10, 11, 39, 40, 43

education 19, 31, 32, 33, 34
Eminescu, Mihai 29
employment 4, 26, 29, 34, 40, 41, 42
environmental issues 47
ethnic groups 25, 26, 27, 34
European Union 4, 11, 19, 29, 35, 37, 38, 41, 42, 43, 47
farming 4, 32, 35, 39, 41, 42
First World War 8, 18
flag 15, 18
food 35, 36, 37, 38
football 30, 32
forests 14, 47
Funar, Gheorghe 18
government 11, 22, 26, 29, 38, 40, 47
Hungary 5, 7, 8, 9, 12, 25, 35, 44
Iasi 18, 24, 28
industry 9, 20, 21, 42, 47
language 5, 25, 29, 30, 33, 34
life expectancy 26
Mamaia 44
Maramures 44
meat 35, 36, 37
Michael the Brave 6
Mihai, King 9, 10
Moldavia 5, 6, 7, 9, 12, 13, 14, 18, 42, 44
music 26, 30, 42
national anthem 15
national parks 47
NATO 4, 11
oil 21, 42
Orthodox Church 7, 27, 37
Ottomans 6, 7, 20

Palace of the Parliament 10, 17
parks 16, 17
Pitesti 20, 22
plants 46, 47
Ploiesti 21
population 9, 12, 16, 18, 21, 25, 26, 27, 28, 39, 42
public transport 32, 41
railways 23, 24
religion 27, 28, 33
rivers 14, 16, 18, 19, 46
roads 22, 23, 41
Roma 26, 32, 34
Romans 5, 18, 45
Russia 4, 7, 8, 9, 10, 14
schools 18, 23, 31, 32, 33, 34
Second World War 4, 5, 9, 10, 11, 16, 21, 27, 39
Serbia 12, 19, 25, 35
shipping 24
Sibiu 21, 24, 45
spa towns 45
Stephen the Great 6
Timisoara 19, 24
Tökés, László 19
tourism 43, 44, 45
Transylvania 5, 6, 7, 8, 9, 14, 18, 21, 25, 26, 39, 43
Ukraine 12, 25, 42, 46
universities 18, 19, 33, 34
Vladimiresci, Tudor 7
Wallachia 5, 6, 7, 14, 16, 18
winter sports 21, 43, 45

ICELAND

N
W   E
S

ATLANTIC OCEAN

NORTH SEA

IRELAND

UNITED
KINGDOM

THE NETHERLAND

BELGIUM

LUXEMBOURG

FRANCE

SWITZERLAN

PORTUGAL   SPAIN

ANDORRA

MEDITERRANE

MOROCCO   ALGERIA

0   500 km

0   500 miles

TUNISIA